ENCOURAGING WORDS

A Source Book of Words
and Phrases for Dissertation
and Report Writers

- Communicate more effectively
- Overcome writer's block
- Find the right phrase
- Sustain motivation
- Avoid repetition

Malinda L. Hayes, Ed.D.

Published in the United States by
Beckham Publications Group, Inc.

ISBN-13: 978-1477657119

10 9 8 7 6 5 4 3 2 1

Encouraging Words

A Source Book of Words and Phrases
for Dissertation and Report Writers

Malinda L. Hayes, Ed.D.

THE Beckham
PUBLICATIONS GROUP, INC.
Silver Spring

Contents

Ten Commandments for Completing the Ph.D.

Thou shall venture into a doctoral program only if thou art motivated and committed to hard work.

Thou shall look to thyself first; success begins there.

Thou shall lay out a written program plan early.

Thou shall stay focused on program milestones.

Thou shall accept and learn from constructive criticism.

Thou shall abide by the rules of the academy, and by all means stay out of campus politics.

Thou shall think small when choosing a dissertation topic area.

Thou shall be aware of personal limitations and be willing to admit that thy might not knoweth everything.

Thou shall consult with thy advisor, a valuable asset.

Thou shall not leave the university until the dissertation is completed.

Howard Adams

Introduction

During the mid-1970s I was an assistant professor at a Northeastern university, assistant director of a community-based outreach educational program, and a doctoral student. In view of all that I was involved in professionally, I was concerned about having enough time to research and write my dissertation. My time management and organizational skills saved me. My determination to succeed gave me the strength to complete the task. I received my degree in 1980.

Since I had been an English teacher I did not anticipate that I would experience much difficulty with writing. However, there were many days and nights (before personal computers) when I found myself sitting at my paper strewn dining room table, unable to move forward with what I thought was a great idea, because I could not think of a phrase or word to express that idea. Sometimes the word or phrase came to me in my sleep. I would wake up, get out of bed, grope about in the dark, and bump into the wall desperately trying to find the light, paper, and pencil to record the word or phrase before it left my mind. I kept all of these notes.

Many times after searching through the notes, I did not use the word or phrase I thought I wanted. Sometimes just looking through the scraps triggered an alternative that I wrote on another scrap of paper and added to my collection. Each time I encountered new words, I wrote them down, and they became a part of the scrap pile.

Consequently, during the process of writing, I accumulated hundreds of scraps of papers with words or phrases written on them. Looking through all of those scraps of papers in an effort to find what I needed became a cumbersome process. To facilitate my search, I tried to collect and organize these tools in a spiral bound, index card notebook with a red cover. I still have that notebook.

My word and phrase collection became my security blanket. It was a source of encouragement for me. As long as I had it, I was never at a loss for words (pun intended).

I still use my little red book when I am researching a subject or writing a report. I have to guard my "encouraging words" notebook because there are people who want it. Some have offered to buy it from me. But I would not sell it. I have allowed a few people to borrow it because they needed encouraging words too.

For many years, I have thought about doing something with my little red book so that I could share it with others who need it. The notion of compiling the notes in it has been on my mind for a long time. Every other year or so I would remind myself that I needed to act on this idea. This is the year. Now is the time for you to have *your own* little red book.

The Purpose

The purpose of this book is to support the writing of students who are at the dissertation stage of their doctoral programs. Although it was compiled for doctoral students, thesis and report writers may find it helpful as well.

Encouraging Words is a prompt to help you think when you encounter writer's block. It is a reference you can use when you cannot call to mind a word or a phrase to communicate your thoughts and ideas effectively.

This book provides opportunities also for learning and vocabulary development. Hopefully it will encourage you to become more aware of words that can be used in academic writing and to compile lists of your own sentences, phrases, and new words.

The lists provide a variety of choices that can help you avoid the repetition of words and phrases that can make your writing seem redundant.

Writing a dissertation can be a lonely and intimidating process. There will be days of frustration and doubt. On those days be sure to read the encouraging words on each page. Let them motivate you and sustain you.

Organization

Most doctoral dissertations in the social sciences share five common structural characteristics.

- Generally, they contain a statement that explains the purpose of the research.
- A research question is conceptualized and defined.
- The research design and methodology for responding to the research questions are developed and explained.
- A literature search based on a review of studies that have been done on the question is compiled and reported.
- Then a discussion and analysis of the literature on the topic, the methodology used for your study and the results of your research are prepared and recorded.

The organization of this book reflects the structural pattern of many doctoral dissertations.

Section I gives you phrases to help you state the purpose of the research.

Section II provides phrases to help you write the literature review.

Section III lists verbs useful for introducing citations of authors' works.

Section IV contains words and phrases applicable to analysis, interpretation, discussion, summary, and conclusions of the study.

The words and phrases in Section V can be helpful in making transitions.

Section VI provides nouns related to research terminology.

Getting The Most Out of This Book

For best results, adopt this book. Give it a home in your briefcase or book-bag. Keep it with you at all times. Let it be a learning experience for you. *Write in it.* Although most of the words in this book will be familiar to you, you will encounter some words that you don't know. Don't give up your dictionary and thesaurus. Make a note of the new words and phrases you meet in your classes and in your reading. Look up new words and record them. As you conduct your literature review, take note of how other writers express themselves. Become aware of the words and phrases they use. Begin your own list of favorite words, and phrases. Use them often enough and they will become yours.

Nothing in this book is written in stone! Take a flexible approach to using this book. The simplest way to use this book is to select the words, phrases, and sentences as they are presented from the lists. However, it is more challenging and creative to use the lists to spark your imagination and reassemble the phrases and sentences by adding or deleting some of the words, by rearranging their order or by developing your own. Record your creations in your notes and use them in your writing. The examples below will clarify this point.

For the example, I have selected the phrase:

Another point of view has been advanced by

To use this phrase as it is presented simply requires you to add an author's name, a school of thought or a group.

Authors: Another point of view has been advanced by **Smith and Jones.**

School of thought: Another point of view has been advanced by **Behaviorists.**

Group: Another point of view has been advanced by **sociologists.**

Here are some variations that can be created from the original phrase.

Behaviorists put forth an opposing viewpoint.

Behaviorist assumptions promote Smith's views.

Smith's work furthers the behaviorist perspective.

To facilitate your getting the most out of this book, the lists of words, phrases, and sentences are arranged alphabetically.

Although the lists are categorized by sections and for use in specific parts of the dissertation, feel free to cross boundaries.Words, phrases, and sentences suggested for use in the literature review can be used also in analysis, discussion, summary, conclusion, and the citation of the work of other writers. Some are introductory phrases. Some are helpful in making transitions, and others are useful in citing studies.

This book is not designed to help you with grammar or sentence structure. When you use the list of verbs and phrases, you must use the appropriate form, tense, and voice. Make sure that subject and verb agree.

Writing a research paper is different from writing an essay. A certain writing style is considered appropriate for research studies. If writing is not one of your strong suits, take heed of what Howard Adams says: *"Thou shall be aware of personal limitations and be willing to admit that thy might not knoweth everything."* When you need help, admit it and run, don't walk, to your nearest human resource, your advisor.

For style and format guidelines refer to your institution's manual of choice.

As you look at the lists of phrases, you will see blank spaces at the beginning of some of them. There will be spaces in the middle of some of them. Some will have blank spaces near the end of them. Sometimes an author's name, a field of study, the name of a specific study or theory, a technique, or your ideas will fill in the blanks. The following examples might be helpful to you.

Blank space at the beginning

Phrase: _____ has been the subject of

Example: Physical attractiveness has been the subject of numerous researchers interested in its impact on the matching theory of interpersonal attraction.

Blank space in the middle

Phrase: The ideas expressed by _____ lead to a broader conceptualization of

Example: The ideas expressed by Jones lead to a broader conceptualization of the matching hypothesis in interpersonal attraction theories.

Blank space near the end

Phrase: Most of the literature suggests that there is some relationship between _____ and _____ .

Example: Most of the literature suggests that there is some relationship between physical attractiveness and dating frequency.

Dissertation–A written thesis that describes the problem, research and findings associated with the independent project conducted by a graduate student after completing course work and general examinations. The dissertation will vary in form and length depending on the discipline and the nature of the research project. It usually requires one to three years to complete. The dissertation is intended to show mastery of knowledge and research tools. It should contribute something new to the discipline in which it is written.

Howard Adams

I. Stating The Purpose of Your Research

Through the years, as a doctoral student and as an employee and administrator in academic institutions, I have had the opportunity to read and review many dissertations. While there are variations, most doctoral dissertations that I have seen contain a statement that identifies the research area, and the purpose of the study, which might include also the question or problem under investigation. This section provides examples of some common expressions used in stating the purpose of research studies. Let them inspire you as you work on constructing your purpose statement.

Example: The primary concern of this research is to examine the effects of sex and race upon the perception of physical attractiveness and social desirability.

In attempting to investigate factors which may account for _____ , this study raises three interrelated questions . . .

The current study investigates the relationship between . . .

The focus of this study will be on . . .

The main purpose of this study is . . .

The objective of this research is to determine . . .

The present study is designed to examine . . .

The primary goal of this study is . . .

The primary concern of this research is . . .

The principal objective of this study is . . .

Quit thinking about all the reasons why you "can't" do something and think of all the reasons you "can."

Glen Bland

The purpose of this study is to address the problem of . . .

The purpose of the present study is . . .

The purpose of this study is to advance understanding of . . .

The purpose of this study is to determine . . .

The purpose of this study is to develop a conceptual model . . .

The purpose of this study is to evaluate . . .

The purpose of this study is to explore the . . .

The purpose of this study is to examine and better understand the effects of . . .

The purpose of this study is to inventory . . .

The purpose of this study is twofold. First, this study will assess the . . .

This research concentrates on . . .

The research problem for this study is to describe the . . .

The specific objectives of the present study are . . .

This study examines the relationships among . . .

There are several reasons for inquiring into . . .

This dissertation explores the idea . . .

This dissertation will deal with . . .

This investigation will explore . . .

> It is our attitude at the beginning of a difficult undertaking which more than anything else will determine its successful outcome.
>
> William James

This investigation represents an attempt to address several . . .

This paper is concerned with . . .

This paper will focus on . . .

This research represents an investigation into the problem of . . .

This research represents an attempt to test the effectiveness of . . .

This study examines . . .

This study has two purposes . . .

This study is concerned with . . .

This study is an attempt to . . .

This study is based on several assumptions . . .

This study is designed to replicate . . .

> If you have no confidence in self,
> you are twice defeated in the race of life.
> With confidence you have won even before
> you have started.
>
> Marcus Garvey

You're not going to accumulate knowledge and experience without taking a few knocks. You're going to meet people who will discourage you, you're going to have to make some choice about what's important, you're going to encounter some things that in the end you will reject because they're false.

You're going to have to be ready to meet those tough times with determination, with a passion for what you're going after, and you're going to have to find people who will say,

"Yes, you should do this, and you can."

Believe me. 'Cause I've done all that.

Bertice Berry

II. The Literature Review

The most difficult task I faced in writing my dissertation was clearly conceptualizing the topic of my research. The ideas I had were fuzzy and very broad. It was not until I began researching the literature that I was able to narrow my topic and develop a research proposal that was realistic and feasible.

Reading the literature and writing the literature review taught me what I needed to know about my topic. I discovered who the pioneers were in the field and what they studied. I was able to trace the chronological and theoretical development of my subject. I learned the issues on which most of the research had been done, and identified areas where more research was needed. Studying the content and structure of the hypotheses and methodologies reported in the literature helped me construct the hypotheses and develop the methodology for my study. The literature review is the foundation of your research.

> The literature review, unlike preceding sections, contains a discussion and explanation of the pertinent documents and analyses of previous inquirers. Controversies, ambiguities and patterns of inquiry in this area of research should be documented in this section.
>
> Charles R. Doty, 1992

The following phrases can be used to help you with the writing of your literature review. If you look at them carefully, you will be able to extract some ideas that will help you organize what you find in your reading.

Feel free to manipulate these phrases to form sentences. Use them at any logical point within a sentence that you are composing. Break them up. Mix and match words to help you express what you want to say.

Phrases Referring To The Literature As A Body, And To General Trends

_____ has been the subject of . . .

A basic assumption, pertinent to the study of _____ is . . .

A number of hypotheses concerning the nature of _____ has been advanced by various authors.

A number of practices currently operative in _____ are designed to . . .

A number of recent experiments have demonstrated . . .

A number of recent studies of _____ are based on _____ 's study of . . .

A number of studies have shown . . .

A recurrent theme in the literature is . . .

A review of the literature illustrates . . .

A significantly high proportion of the studies in the field are concerned with . . .

A substantial body of research reveals . . .

A succinct review of . . .

According to . . .

According to most of the literature produced on this subject, there . . .

Accumulating research indicates . . .

Don't waste life in doubts and fears, spend yourself on the work before you, well assured that the right performance of this hour's duties will be the best preparation for the hours or ages that follow it.

Ralph Waldo Emerson

There are three questions to be answered in the literature review:

(1) What is the essential literature on this problem?

(2) What patterns of inquiry are present in the literature? and

(3) How does the inquiry proposed for this study logically follow these patterns of inquiry?

Charles R. Doty 1992

Adherents to the theory of . . .

Among current trends in the study of . . .

An area which needs to be explored . . .

An indication of the importance attached to the study of _____ is . . .

An examination of . . .

An interesting hypothesis . . .

Another aspect of . . .

Another point of view has been advanced by . . .

Another point of view has been discussed by . . .

As noted in . . .

As noted previously . . .

Assumptions can be extracted from the current research literature.

We must not become discouraged.

Booker T. Washington

Attention should be directed toward . . .

Central to . . .

Characteristically, these studies examined . . .

Crucial to . . .

Earlier research findings show . . .

Evidence regarding the . . .

Few investigations have evaluated . . .

Findings of earlier studies generally agree with . . .

General trends are apparent in the studies cited in . . .

Highly critical to . . .

Impetus for . . .

In reviewing the research literature . . .

In terms of the theory under review . . .

In the review of the literature, _____ will be discussed.

Interest has been generated in . . .

It has been noted that . . .

It is only recently that researchers have begun to examine
systematically the effect of . . .

I refused to be discouraged, for neither

God nor man could use a discouraged soul.

Mary McLeod Bethune

More attention is being devoted to . . .

Most of the literature suggests that there is some relationship between _____ and _____ .

Most researchers on the subject of . . .

Most writers have ignored . . .

Of relevance here is the research of _____

One of the central questions of the current studies is . . .

Other researchers have demonstrated . . .

Pertinent to . . .

Previous research findings show . . .

Previous research has investigated the impact of _____ upon _____ .

Previous research, utilizing various methodologies, indicated a significant relationship between _____ and _____ .

Research in _____ has passed through various stages in its development.

Research investigating _____ has revealed . . .

Recent investigations continue to interpret . . .

Recent studies reveal. . .

Research up to this point has . . .

Researchers have given little theoretical attention to. . .

Researchers have raised questions about . . .

> Always believe that what you do today is in preparation for something better tomorrow.
>
> Samuel D. Proctor

Several assumptions can be deduced from the current research literature.

Several researchers have noted . . .

Several researchers take the position that . . .

Several studies point out . . .

Some long standing assumptions of _____ have been questioned.

Some researchers argue that . . .

Studies have investigated . . .

Studies of _____ and its relationship to _____ highlight . . .

Subsequent inquiries have . . .

Tangential to . . .

The argument that _____ is an effective technique is well documented.

The contention that _____ is an effective _____ is well documented.

The crux of the matter is . . .

The greatest research effort on this issue has been to . . .

The hypothesis of _____ was initially tested by _____

The ideas expressed by _____ lead to a broader conceptualization of . . .

The largest proportion of the studies support the premise . . .

The leading exponent of . . .

> Keep your eyes on the prize,
> Hold on, hold on.
>
> Traditional civil rights song

The literature is replete with references to . . .

The literature reveals a diversity of opinions on . . .

The literature review will focus on . . .

The most notable _____ about . . .

The notion of _____ is supported by the research of . . .

The question arises . . .

The review of the literature is instructive in . . .

The studies cited in . . .

The subject of _____ has received minimal attention.

Theoretical advances have . . .

Theoretical speculations about . . .

There are several reasons for inquiring into . . .

There has been little investigation of . . .

There is a growing body of evidence that shows . . .

There is also documentation of . . .

These outcomes can be generalized to . . .

These studies indicate . . .

This interest has not been limited to . . .

This point of view is rapidly gaining support.

People will know you're serious when you produce.

Muhammad Ali

This thesis was initially explored by . . .

This topic is in need of further study and clarification.

Within the context of . . .

With few exceptions . . .

A recent study by _____

A study by _____ advances the notion that . . .

A study by _____ supports this hypothesis.

A study by _____ puts forth . . .

A study concerned specifically with _____ is _____'s investigation of

_____'s study gave priority to . . .

Another writer who explored _____

_____ as described by

Based on the results of interviews with subjects in her study,

_____ proposed . . . _____

_____ , in a more recent study

In his discussion of_____ , _____ reported

_____ is described by _____ as

No one has stated this position as clearly as _____

Other studies conducted by _____ substantiate . . .

The purpose of a study conducted by _____

Go PLACIDLY amid the noise and the haste, and remember what peace there may be in silence. As far as possible without surrender be on good terms with all persons. Speak your truth quietly and clearly; and listen to others.

Anonymous

This study considered . . .

_____ was more detailed and explicit in defining . . .

_____'s work is based on the earlier research of . . .

_____'s work is pertinent to this school of thought.

> One generation plants the trees; another gets the shade.
>
> Chinese Proverb

Phrases To Use With Author's Name And To Cite Studies

In reviewing the literature, you will become aware of the researchers who have contributed knowledge to the topic you are studying. In reporting these contributions, you will want to do more than just simply summarize or quote the work of earlier researchers. It is feasible to point out how they affected the discipline.

These phrases can help you describe the nature of their contribution. I encourage you to manipulate them to serve your purposes. They can be used with an author's name and to cite the outcome of studies. The following examples will illustrate the possibilities.

Example phrase: displayed indifference to

Example: Until recently social scientists have displayed systematic indifference to physical attractiveness as a legitimate sociological concern.

Example: Jones was indifferent to sociologists' early assumptions regarding physical attractiveness as a legitimate theoretical concern.

Example: Jones' studies challenge sociologists' indifference to physical attractiveness as a legitimate area of scholarly inquiry.

_____ advanced the notion of . . .

_____ affirmed the fact . . .

_____ affirmed the work of. . .

_____ arrived at the conclusion in her study that . . .

_____ attested to . . .

If there is no struggle, there is no progress.

Frederick Douglas

_____ called attention to . . .

_____ cited the need for . . .

_____ clarified the point that . . .

_____ commenting on _____ explained . . .

_____ concentrated on . . .

_____ conducted a study of . . .

_____ developed the conceptual framework for . . .

_____ discovered in his studies that . . .

_____ discussed the problem of . . .

_____ displayed indifference to . . .

_____ drew a parallel between . . .

_____ elaborated further and revealed that . . .

_____ emphasized the plausibility of . . .

_____ established a connection between . . .

_____ established a connection to . . .

_____ established a convincing case . . .

_____ examined the effect of . . .

_____ executed a study on . . .

Do well today on account of tomorrow.

African Proverb

_____ explored the subject of . . .

_____ expressed the view of

_____ failed to consider . . .

_____ failed to consider some facts directly germane to . . .

_____ focused on

_____ gave attention to . . .

_____ gave a description of

_____ gave cognizance to . . .

_____ gave credence to

_____ has shown . . .

_____ highlighted another problem . . .

_____ identified and reported

_____ identified the problem of . . .

_____ illustrated the problems of . . .

_____ in a more recent study, explored . . .

_____ inquired into . . .

_____ introduced the idea of . . .

> What we obtain too cheap, we esteem too lightly; it is dearness only that gives everything its value
>
> Thomas Paine

_____ noted a dominant focus in the literature on . . .

_____ noted a major discrepancy . . .

_____ offered the hypothesis . . .

_____ pointed out . . .

_____'s premise . . .

_____ presented a clear explanation of . . .

_____ presented a strong argument . . .

_____ presented an account of . . .

_____ presented a description of . . .

_____ presented evidence of . . .

_____ proceeded to detail . . .

_____ produced information concerning . . .

_____ provided an explanation of . . .

_____ provided a detailed analysis of . . .

_____ provided information on . . .

_____ provided some insights into . . .

_____ put forth . . .

Wealth, if you use it, comes to an end;
Learning, if you use it, increases.

Swahili Proverb

_____ raised the question of . . .

_____ reached a similar conclusion . . .

_____ reached this conclusion based on . . .

_____ reached this conclusion on the basis of his investigation of . . .

_____ referred to . . .

_____ referred to this process as . . .

_____ reflected this view when he wrote . . .

_____ relied upon . . .

_____ reported positive results for . . .

_____ researched the subject of _____ and learned . . .

_____'s review of _____ documented . . .

_____ shared insights into . . .

_____'s suggestion . . .

_____ summarized the evidence accurately and
        discussed the problem of . . .

_____'s survey of . . .

_____ tested the effectiveness of . . .

_____ tested the hypothesis . . .

Two roads diverged in a wood, and I . . .

I took the one less traveled by,

And that has made all the difference.

Robert Frost

_____ tested the impact of _____on _ _____ and found . . .

_____ tested the effectiveness of _____

_____ tested the hypothesis . . .

_____ took the position that . . .

_____ underscored the feasibility of . . .

_____ was concerned with . . .

_____ was critical of . . .

When you begin a great work, you can't expect to finish it all at once; therefore do you and your brothers press on, and let nothing discourage you until you have entirely finished what you have begun.

Teedyuscung, Delaware

III. Words for Citations

A s you write your dissertation, you will be citing studies written by authors in your discipline. My list helped me to avoid overusing the same words to credit my sources. In using these words, you will have to decide when to change them into other parts of speech.

For an example, I have chosen the word, develop.

Verb: Jones developed a more explicit definition of the term.

Noun: Jones' development resulted in a more explicit definition of the term.

Adjective: A developing body of research by Jones and his colleagues clarified the definition of the term.

accomplish
account
acknowledge
adapt
address
admit
adopt
advance
advocate
affirm

agree
align
alleviate
allude
ameliorate
amplify
analyze
anticipate
apply
appraise

approach
argue
articulate

> If you have learning, you'll never lose your way.
>
> Yiddish Proverb

ascertain
ascribe
assert
assess
associate
assume
attain
attend to
attenuate
attest
attribute
believe
caution
censure
challenge
circumvent
cite
clarify
coincide
comment
compare
compound
comprise

concede
conceive
concentrate
conceptualize
conclude
concretize
concur
confine
confirm
confound
confront
consider
constitute
contaminate
contemplate
contend
contest
contrast
contribute
convey
correlate
corroborate
counter

create
credit
crystallize
culminate
declare
deduce
defend
define
delineate
demonstrate
denote
depict
derive
describe
design

> Never let your head hang down. Never give up and sit and grieve. Find another way. And don't pray when it rains if you don't pray when the sun shines.
>
> Satchel Paige

designate
detail
deter
determine
devaluate
develop
devise
dichotomize
differentiate
digress
disagree
discern
disclose
discover
discredit
discuss
dispel
disseminate
dissipate
distinguish
effectuate
elaborate
elucidate

emanate
emphasize
employ
encapsulate
encourage
endeavor
endemic
engender
enlighten
ensue
ensure
entail
enumerate
envisage
envision
establish
evaluate
eventuate
exacerbate
examine
explain
explore
express

extol
extract
extrapolate
facilitate
find
foreshadow
formulate
foster
generate
highlight
hypothesize
identify
illustrate
impede
imply

Talk without effort is nothing.

Maria W. Stewart

32

impute
include
incorporate
inculcate
indicate
induce
indulge
infringe
integrate
internalize
interpret
intervene
interview
intimate
introduce
investigate
involve
justify
juxtapose
know
learn
legitimize
link

maintain
manifest
mention
modify
note
notice
obscure
observe
offer
opine
opposed
overlook
permeate
perpetuate
persist
peruse
pervade
postulate
precede
preclude
predict
predispose
prepare

presuppose
proceed
proclaim
produce
promulgate
propose
propound
proselytize
provide
pursue
qualify
question
realign
realize
reason

To get where you want to go you can't only do what you like.

Peter Abrahams

recognize
recommend
reconcile
reevaluate
refer
reflect
refute
regard
reinforce
reiterate
relate
remark
render
replicate
report
represent
rescind
research
resolve
restrict
revamp
reveal
review

say
scrutinize
secure
show
speak
speculate
state
stress
study
substantiate
suggest
summarize
superimpose
supplant
support
surmise
surmount
survey
sustain
test
theorize
transcend
transform

typify
underscore
understand
validate
verify
view
vitiate
witness
write

I have fought a good fight,

I have finished my course,

I have kept the faith.

New Testament, II Timothy 4:7

IV. Words And Phrases For Summaries, Analysis And Discussion

Throughout your research and your writing, you look critically and analytically at the research in your field.

> The relevant studies need to be critiqued rather than reported. The critique serves to inform the reader about the status of reliable knowledge in the field and to identify errors to avoid in future research.
>
> Kjell E. Rudeston & Rac R. Newton, 1992

You will find the following to be helpful:

a basic assumption throughout this analysis . . .

a clear report of . . .

a closer inspection of these assumptions suggests . . .

a distinct tendency to . . .

a necessary but not sufficient condition . . .

a parallel analysis . . .

a similar finding was reported by . . .

> Without faith a man can do nothing: with it all things are possible.
>
> Sir William Osler

a strong argument in favor of this point is . . .

a variant of this justification . . .

absence of opportunity . . .

absence of proof . . .

adequate base for . . .

adhere to the basic principles of . . .

adherence to formalized procedures . . .

adversely affected . . .

affinity between . . .

Although the studies that are cited do not _____ , they do reveal . . .

an analysis of . . .

An exception is provided by _____ who explored the effect of _____ on _____ .

An important theoretical assumption . . .

An interesting hypothesis . . .

An unexpected consequence of . . .

_____ and _____ are apparently interrelated . . .

analytical clarity . . .

analytical framework . . .

> No matter how long the night, the day is sure to come.
>
> Congo

analytically perceptive . . .

Another aspect of . . .

Another phenomenon that may be closely related to _____ is . . .

_____ arrived at the conclusion in this study that . . .

are legitimate aspects . . .

As you read the available research in an area, you need to maintain a critical perspective, evaluating the study on its own merits and in comparison to other studies on the same or similar problems.

Kjell E. Rudeston & Rae R. Newton, 1992

---

are obviously interrelated . . .

areas delineated for further research . . .

Arguments for the significance of _____ have become . . .

arising out of . . .

ascribed relationship . . .

attempt to estimate . . .

attempt to extract . . .

attribute to . . .

basic components . . .

basic hypothesis expounded upon . . .

Education is our passport to the future, for tomorrow belongs to the people who prepare for it today.

Malcolm X

basic to . . .

can be generalized . . .

can be estimated . . .

can be inferred from . . .

can be justified . . .

catalytic role . . .

categorical and rigid judgment . . .

centrality in . . .

certain limitations seem apparent . . .

closer inspection of . . .

circumstances are incompatible . . .

codification of . . .

coherent conceptual framework . . .

complex issue . . .

complicity between . . .

conceptual aspects . . .

conclusion of this analysis . . .

conspicuously absent . . .

constitutive elements . . .

Hope is the pillar of the world.

African Proverb

corresponds to . . .

could argue reasonably . . .

critical intervention

critically analyzes . . .

conducive to . . .

consideration of . . .

contingent upon . . .

convergence of . . .

coterminous with . . .

critical distinction . . .

correlative emphasis . . .

Data provided by preceding studies tend to support . . .

deflection of criticism . . .

denial of the importance of . . .

departs from . . .

derives from . . .

deriving primary definition, characteristics and form from . . .

deserves further examination . . .

determinants of . . .

The difference between failure and success is doing a thing nearly right and doing a thing exactly right.

Edward Simmons

diametrically opposed to . . .

differentiated from . . .

differentiated sets of relationships . . .

direct causal relationship . . .

directly attributable to . . .

directly germane to . . .

discuss conceptually . . .

disparity between . . .

dispel the prevalent notion of . . .

disposition for . . .

distinct tendency . . .

diverse reactions . . .

diversity of viewpoints . . .

dynamic processes . . .

elements to consider . . .

endemic to . . .

essential dimensions . . .

evidence indicates . . .

Start with what you know and build
on what you have.

Kwame Nkrumah

evidence pertinent to . . .

exclusionary forces . . .

extensive data . . .

extraneous factors . . .

failed to find support for . . .

far reaching ramifications . . .

A critique does not imply that you must discover and identify a major flaw or weakness in every study you read. You are evaluating the content for its application to your research.

Kjell E. Rudeston & Rae R. Newton, 1992

follows a predictable course . . .

formulate several hypotheses . . .

found no evidence for . . .

from his viewpoint . . .

functional requirement of . . .

fundamental analytical requirement . . .

fundamental aspect . . .

fundamental objective . . .

The day on which one starts out is not the time to start one's preparation.

Nigeria

fundamentally conflicting outcomes . . .

general application of . . .

general neglect of . . .

Generally, these reactions have taken several forms.

Given _____ , it is possible that . . .

Given the evidence, . . .

Given the preceding context . . .

has consequences in . . .

has great strategic value . . .

has a validity . . .

has particular relevance to . . .

has some bearing on the broader issues of . . .

has received minimal attention . . .

having no intrinsic relationship to . . .

Herein lies one of the reasons.

Implicit in the theoretical analysis of _____ is the . . .

Implicit in the notion of _____ is the basic assumption that . . .

impractical consideration . . .

Anticipate the good so that you may enjoy it.

Ethiopian Proverb

In a fundamental sense . . .

In conclusion . . .

in conflict and irreconcilable . . .

in conjunction with . . .

in further consideration of . . .

in further recognition of . . .

in need of further study . . .

in order to extend the scope of . . .

in recognition of . . .

In summary . . .

in the absence of . . .

In view of the close connection between _____ and _____ . . .

In view of these considerations, . . .

incumbent upon . . .

indispensable conditions . . .

indisputably clear . . .

indistinguishable from . . .

Inspection of the data reveals . . .

interpretive analysis of . . .

> You have the ability, now apply yourself.
>
> Benjamin Mays

interpretive analysis of some key_____ issues . . .

intrinsic relationship . . .

investigators continue to interpret . . .

irrespective of . . .

is confined to . . .

is derived from . . .

is prone to . . .

is representative of . . .

is subordinate to . . .

It is conceivable that . . .

It is evident that . . .

It is important to consider . . .

It is important to note . . .

It is questionable whether . . .

It is reasonable to assume . . .

It should be noted that . . .

leads to investigation . . .

logical aspects . . .

major implications of . . .

People who are unable to motivate themselves must be content with mediocrity no matter how impressive their other talents.

Andrew Carnegie

major point . . .

major tenet . . .

make a convincing case . . .

make some assessment of . . .

markedly discrepant data . . .

methodological consideration . . .

might be interpreted as . . .

modal consequences . . .

more detailed analysis . . .

mutual relevance . . .

objectively verifiable . . .

obscured from accurate appraisal . . .

obvious flow . . .

on the basis of these findings . . .

offer an explanation of . . .

operational significance . . .

over simplification . . .

phenomena related to . . .

pervasive influence . . .

When things go wrong as they sometimes will,
When the road you're trudging seems all up hill,
When the funds are low and the debts are high,
And you want to smile, but you have to sigh,
When care is pressing you down a bit,
Rest if you must——but don't you quit.

Clinton Howell

point of departure . . .

points not limited to . . .

predicated upon . . .

presents the problem of . . .

problems not central to . . .

proposes as fundamental . . .

qualifying elements . . .

qualitative analysis . . .

quantitative analysis . . .

question the appropriateness of . . .

questions that challenge . . .

ramifications . . .

reasonable interpretation . . .

reciprocal relationship . . .

reciprocal roles . . .

Recognition of this phenomenon raises the possibility that . . .

recognize the basic concepts . . .

recognize the essential concepts . . .

recognizes no distinction . . .

I hear and I forget.

I see and I remember.

I do and I understand.

Asian Proverb

re-conceptualize . . .

re-examine essential concepts . . .

recurrent patterns . . .

recurrent themes . . .

relationships that seem to have the greatest credibility . . .

relative consistency . . .

relative frequency . . .

replicate . . .

representative sample . . .

require reflection and scrutiny . . .

results suggest . . .

run counter to . . .

seem to operate differentially . . .

set limits . . .

sets of relationships . . .

Several reasons account for . . .

significant outcome . . .

simplistic formulation of the problem . . .

sole criterion . . .

> All things are possible until they are proved impossible — even the impossible may only be so, as of now.
>
> Pearl S. Buck

some parallels are readily apparent . . .

Some questions have been raised about the conditions and extent of . . .

sound and coherent theory . . .

sporadic efforts . . .

spurious effects . . .

state of dynamic interaction . . .

stemming from this conclusion . . .

substantiate . . .

subsumed under the term, . . .

susceptible to . . .

systematic and purposeful . . .

systematically formulated . . .

tend to be associated with . . .

the basic correlates are . . .

The complexities involved in . . .

The concept of _____ is linked to _____ . . .

The effectiveness of . . .

The findings of earlier studies appear to be in
   general agreement with _____ .

The secret of achievement is not to let what you're doing get to you before you get to it.

Anonymous

The focus can be . . .

The general theoretical context of _____ is assumed to be fundamental to . . .

The kinds of questions raised in this analysis . . .

The largest proportion of studies support the premise . . .

The major implications of . . .

The notion that _____ remains tenable.

The present analysis will draw upon . . .

The resolution of this contradiction . . .

The results of this study should be interpreted after consideration of the following limitations . . .

The results run counter to . . .

The results were consistent with . . .

The significance of . . .

The study's findings suggest . . .

The transition from . . .

The ultimate effect . . .

under scrutiny . . .

underlying dynamics . . .

The underlying rationale . . .

The validity of _____ can be determined by . . .

> Turn what has been done into a better path. If you are a leader, think about the impact of your decisions on seven generations into the future.
>
> Cherokee Traditional Precept

There are similar implications in the findings of . . .

There is ample justification for . . .

There is other evidence which indicates that . . .

There is some basis for concluding . . .

These factors are plausibly related to . . .

These outcomes do not support previously established data.

These tables reflect . . .

This analysis implies . . .

This analysis does not imply . . .

This conclusion does not seem warranted . . .

These findings differ from . . .

This finding should be interpreted as . . .

This is a finding that bears directly on _____ . . .

This pattern persists . . .

This phenomena derives from . . .

This phenomenon may extend to . . .

This phenomenon was explained in terms of . . .

This point is not peculiar to . . .

This prediction ignores . . .

Faith is the substance of things hoped for, and the evidence of things not seen.

New Testament, Hebrews 11:1

This result does coincide with previously published data . . .

This study takes as its interpretative framework . . .

This study's findings suggest . . .

to go unchallenged . . .

token applicability to . . .

ultimate effectiveness . . .

underscored the plausibility . . .

unexpected consequences . . .

underlying commonalties . . .

viable alternative . . .

For they can conquer who believe they can.

Virgil

V. Transitions

Frequently you must move or make the transition from one idea to the next. These transitional words and phrases can be used to help you tie your ideas together

Accordingly
Additionally
Albeit
Although
As a result
By virtue of
Consequently
Conversely
Equally important
Even though
Finally
Fundamentally
Further
Furthermore
Hence
Hereafter
However

Hypothetically
In addition
In comparison
In contrast
In effect
In essence
In fact
In spite of
In summary
In this respect
Moreover
Most noticeably
Nevertheless
Nonetheless
Notwithstanding
On the other hand
Since

Specifically
Thereby
Therefore
Thus
To an extent
To that end
To the contrary
Whereas
With respect to
Yet

The price of your hat isn't the measure of your brain.

Traditional

VI. Nouns Related To Research

This list of nouns is composed of words that are familiar to you but might not come to mind when you need one of them. They are frequently used in research studies and reports. When you can't think of a noun that best suits your needs, let this list stimulate your thoughts.

accuracy

analysis

appraisal

approach

aspect

assessment

assumption

bias

basis

characteristic

cohort

collection

commentary

comparison

complexity

component

concept

conclusion

condition

configuration

consequence

consideration

consistency

content

context

contention

contradiction

controversy

conversion

correlation

credence

credibility

No matter what accomplishment you make, somebody helps you.

Althea Gibson

53

criteria

data

deduction

definition

determinant

development

differentiation

dilemma

dimension

discovery

discrepancy

discussion

disparity

dissimilarity

distribution

documentation

effect

element

etiology

evaluation

evidence

evolution

examination

exclusion

expectation

facet

factors

feasibility

findings

focus

framework

generalization

hypothesis

ideology

impact

implication

inception

inclusion

increment

indication

indicators

influence

initiative

inquiry

intent

interaction

interpretation

intervention

inventory

investigation

justification

limitation

measures

Doing little things well is a step toward doing big things better.

Anonymous

mechanism

methodology

modc

model

modification

norm

notion

outcome

paradigm

paradox

parameter

paucity

perception

perspective

phenomenon

plethora

polarity

population

potential

practices

precept

prediction

premise

principal

principle

procedure

proliferation

proponent

proposal

proposition

ramification

range

rationale

reinforcement

relationship

relevance

reliability

remedy

replication

resolution

resource

respondent

results

sample

significance

statistics

status

study

subjects

survey

tendency

theory

thesis

trait

validity

variable

verification

Everything that has a beginning, has an end.

African Proverb

References

Adams, Howard G. *Making the Grade in Graduate School: Survival Strategy 101*. Notre Dame, IN: The Gem Center, 1993.

Ayalti, Hanan J. *Yiddish Proverbs*. New York: Schocken Books, New Impression Edition, 1987.

Baym, Nina. *The Norton Anthology of American Literature*. New York: WW Norton and Co, Inc, 2002.

Bell, Janet Cheatham *Famous Black Quotations*. (Ed.) New York: Warner, 1995.

Berlin, Ester G. *In the Cycle of the Whirl*. In Simon Ortiz (Ed.) *Speaking for the Generations*. Tucson: University of Arizona Press, 1998.

Berry, Bertice. *I'm on My Way but Your Foot Is on My Head: A Black Woman's Story of Getting Over Life's Hurdles*. New York: Simon and Schuster, 1966.

Bland, Glenn. *Success! The Glenn Bland Method*. Wheaton, IL:Tyndale House Publishers Inc., 1983.

Copage, Eric V. *Black Pearls: Daily Meditations, Affirmations, and Inspirations for African-Americans*. New York: Quill, 1993.

Deane, Elizabeth. *Gentle Thoughts: A Collection of Tender and Wise Sayings from Sundry Authors of Wisdom and Renown*.Mount Vernon, N.Y: Peter Pauper Press, 1983.

Doty, Charles R.. *Guide to Dissertation Proposal and Dissertation Preparation*. New Brunswick, N.J: Graduate School of Education, Rutgers The State University, 1992.

Ehrlich, Eugene, & Debruhl, Marshall (Eds.). *The International Thesaurus of Quotations. Revised edition.* New York: Collins, 1996.

Glazer, Mark. (Ed.). *A Dictionary of Mexican American Proverbs.* New York: Greenwood Press, 1987.

Griffin, Albert Kirby. *Religious Proverbs: Over 1600 Adages from 18 Faiths Worldwide. Jefferson,* Lincoln, NE.: Author's Choice Press, 2001.

Hayes, Malinda L. *The Effect of Sex and Race Upon the Perception of Physical Attractiveness, Social Desirability, and Employability of Women.* (Doctoral dissertation), Rutgers The State University, New Brunswick, N.J. 1980.

Hill, Roberta. *Immersed in Words.* In Simon Ortiz (Ed.), *Speaking for the Generations.* Tucson: University of Arizona Press, 1998.

McKnight, Reginald. *Wisdom of the African World.* Novato, CA: The Classic Wisdom Press, 1996.

Nerburn, Kent and Mengelkock, Louise. *Native American Wisdom.* San Rafael, CA: Classic Wisdom Press, 1991.

Ortiz, Simon (Ed.). *Speaking for the Generations, Native Writers on Writing.* Tucson: University of Arizona Press, 1998.

Rudeston, Kjell Erik and Newton, Rae R. *Surviving Your Dissertation: A Comprehensive Guide to Content and Process.* Newbury Park, CA: Sage Publications, 1992.

Van Ekern, Glenn. *Words for All Occasions.* Paramus, N.J.: Prentice Hall, 1988.

Warner, Carolyn. *Treasury of Women's Quotations.* Englewood Cliffs, N.J.: Prentice Hall, 1997.

Zona, Guy T. *The House of the Heart is Never Full and Other Proverbs of Africa.* New York: Simon and Schuster, 1993.

Your Words Are Important

I hope that Encouraging Words has been an inspiration for you.

Please send any ideas, phrases, words or suggestions that you are willing to share. Let me hear from you.

Malinda L. Hayes
c/o Beckham Publications Group
P.O. Box 4066
Silver Spring, MD 20914